Purple Ronnie's

♡ Little Book for ♡

The World's Best
GIRLFRIEND

by Purple Ronnie

First published 2009 by Boxtree
an imprint of Pan Macmillan Ltd
Pan Macmillan, 20 New Wharf Road, London N1 9RR
Basingstoke and Oxford
Associated companies throughout the world
www.panmacmillan.com

ISBN 978-0-7522-2696-5

9 8 7 6 5 4 3 2

A CIP catalogue record for this book is
available from the British Library.

Printed and bound in Hong Kong

'Purple Ronnie' created by Giles Andreae. The right of Giles Andreae and Janet Cronin
to be identified respectively as the author and illustrator of this work has been asserted by them
in accordance with the Copyright, Designs and Patents Act 1988.

Visit **www.panmacmillan.com** to read more about all our books
and to buy them. You will also find features, author interviews and
news of any author events, and you can sign up for e-newsletters
so that you're always first to hear about our new releases.

Love Poem

I just want to tell you
I love you so much
That each time I look
at your face
My heart jumps a somersault
Round in the air
And my feelings explode
into space

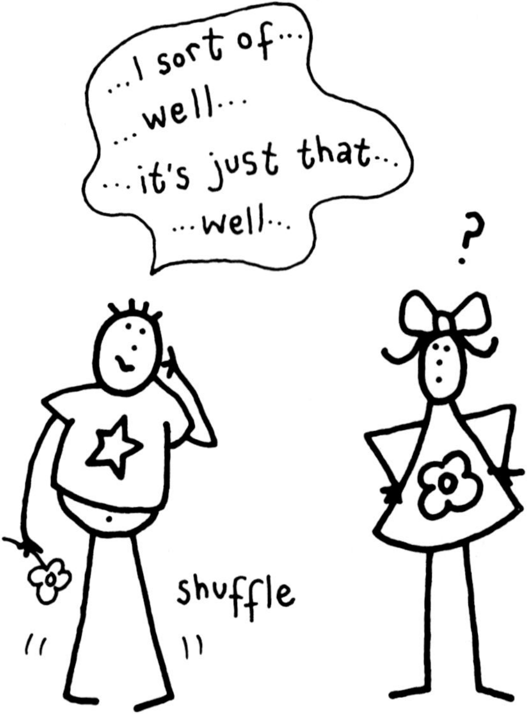
...I sort of...
...well...
...it's just that...
...well...
?
shuffle

My Own Little Way

I sometimes get rather
embarrassed
And don't always know
what to say
When it comes to expressing
my feelings
But I try in my own
little way

Special Tip

Girlfriends never get tired of being told how special they are

a poem to say
I Love You

When I am lying alone
in my bed

All sorts of thoughts
come into my head

Like why do I Love You as
much as I do?

Then I know it's because
you are _You_

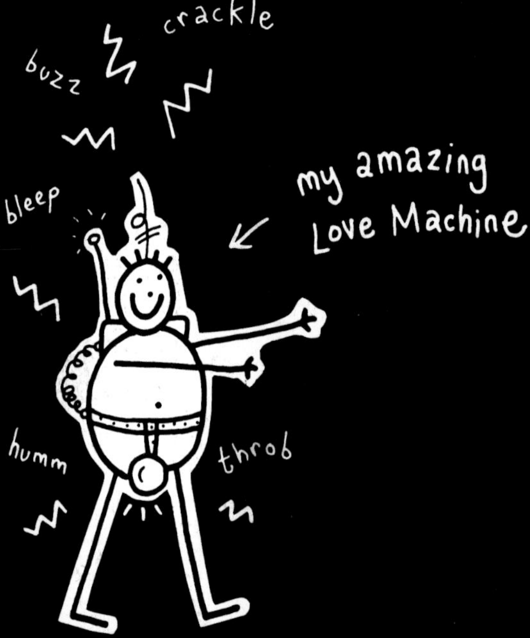
crackle
buzz
my amazing
Love Machine
bleep
humm
throb

a poem for a
Lover

If someone invented a
                    gadget
That made me terrific in
                      bed
I think I'd buy twenty-five
                    thousand
And Do It with you till
                    I'm dead

Beware

Try not to fall out
with your girlfriend's
mates, it could get
you into trouble

a poem to say

You're Lovely

If I was more clever
I would find a special way
To tell you that you're
lovely
Cos that's all I want
to say

a little

Hugging Poem

I want you to know
That I think you are
        great
And although I'm a bit
        of a mug
If you ever need me
I'll always be near
To come round and give you
        a hug

Special Tip

Don't try telling your girlfriend she has too many shoes, she won't know what you mean

a shy poem ↓

To Someone I Like

I sometimes find it rather
hard
To say I really care
And that I like you
quite a lot
But I've said it now —
so there

Your Special Treat

I wanted to do something
                    special for you
I thought that a cake would
                        impress
I'm sure that I did what it
                    said in the book
But I've just made a bloomin'
                    great mess...

Warning

NEVER go rummaging in your girlfriend's handbag - handbags are strictly private

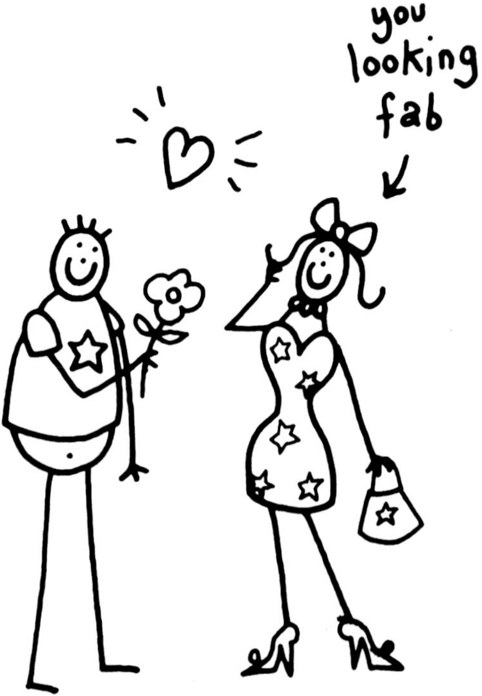
you looking fab

a poem to say

You're Gorgeous

Sometimes as women get
older
Their bodies start showing
the weather

Their things start to droop
and to dangle

But you look more gorgeous
than ever!

The Hairdresser

Whenever you've been to the
hairdresser
WOWZA! Well don't you look hot!

It's great you come back looking
lovely

But why must it cost such
alot?

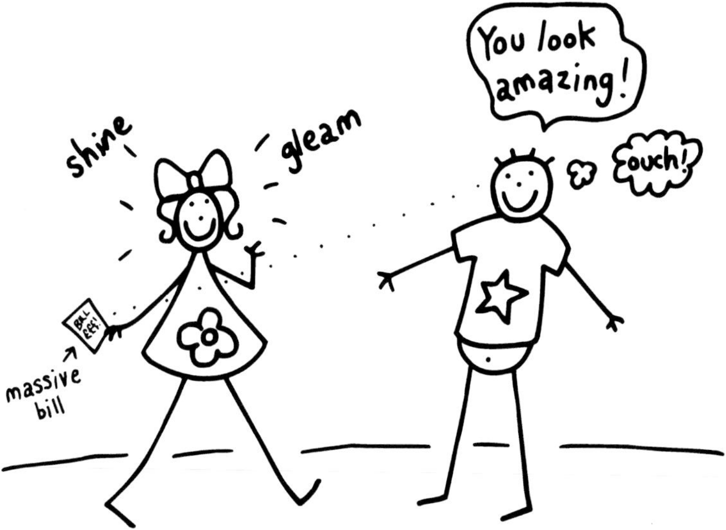
shine
gleam
BILL
£££!
massive bill
You look amazing!
ouch!

Beware

Sometimes a girlfriend may need to try on a dozen outfits to decide the first was alright

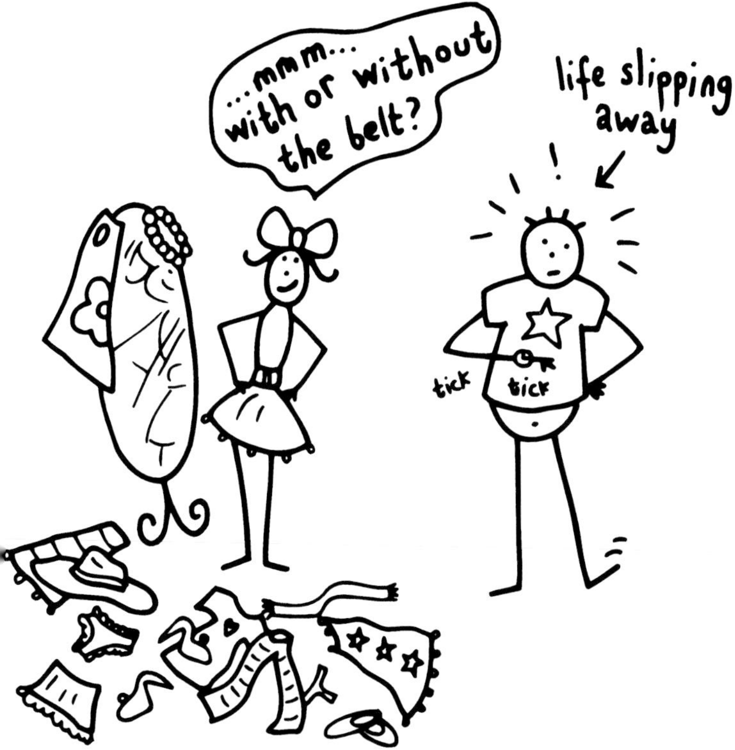
...mmm...
with or without
the belt?
life slipping
away
tick
tick

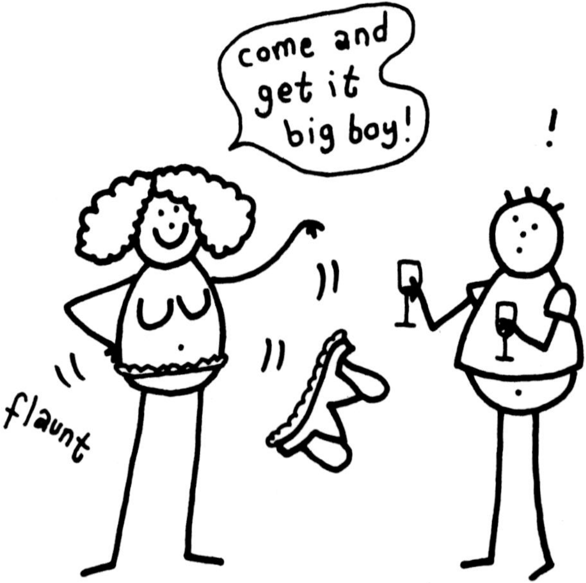
come and get it big boy!
!
flaunt

a poem about
↓
Girls

Some girls hide under the
duvet
Then peel off their clothes
bit by bit
But others love flaunting
their gorgeous basoomers
And instantly dropping
their kit

a poem about
Saucy Undies

I bought you the sexiest
knickers
In the hope that you'd preen
and you'd pose
But when you unwrapped them
And saw what I'd got
You giggled "I'm not wearing THOSE!"

Special Tip

Some girlfriends like to teach their boyfriends new tricks.

Be Prepared!

a poem about

That Tingly Feeling

It starts in the tips of
your fingers

And moves to the end of
your nose

And then it starts zooming
all over the place

Till it fills you right down
to your toes

Shouting Names

Some people get turned on if you shout out their name while you're Doing It...

... make sure you know
what they are called first.

Special Tip

Some girlfriends love a romantic dinner...
which they haven't had to cook

a poem to say

You're Scrumptious

However much money I pay
people
Some of them still won't
agree
That you're almost as
wonderfully scrumptious
And gorgeously smashing
as me!

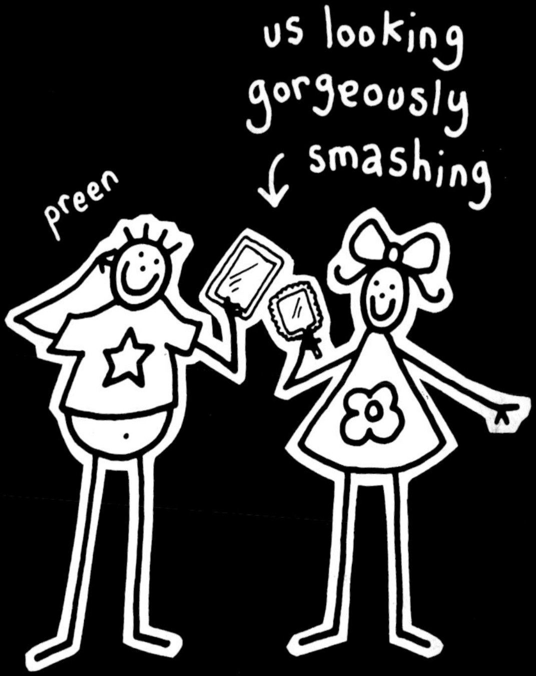
us looking gorgeously smashing
preen

a poem about

True Love

I want you to know that
I love you

And to prove that my feelings
are true

I'll give up this Saturday's footie

And even come shopping with
you!

Special Tip

If your girlfriend asks you if her bum looks big in this **ALWAYS** say no

a poem about ↓

Fantasies

Some girls dream they'll
fall in love
With aliens from Mars
But others just want
rampant sex
With oily men in
cars

a poem about

My Girl

My heart is really hopping
My head is in a whirl
I can't believe I heard
                    you right—
You want to be my girl !

Beware

Girlfriends can sometimes turn very moody. When this happens, it is best to stay out of their way!

about to explode
ggrrrr
fizz
crackle
spark
Right, see you in a bit then
scarper

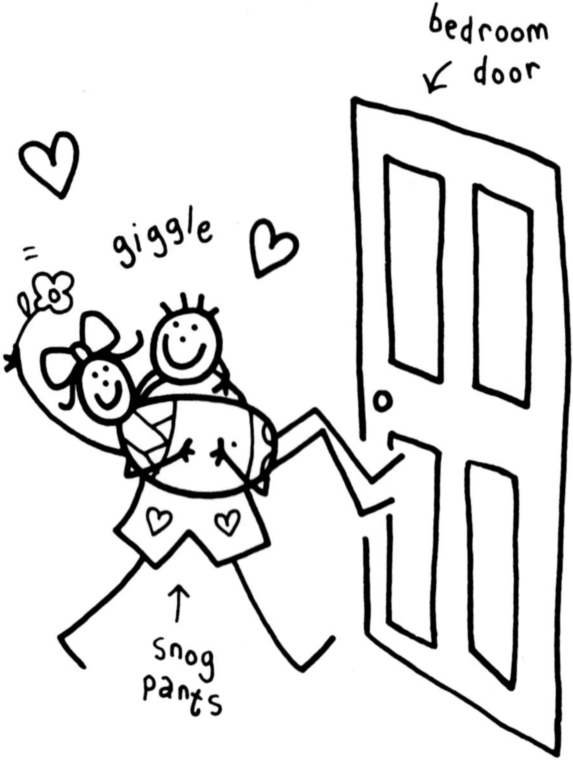
bedroom door
giggle
snog pants

a little
Love Poem
(arrow pointing down between "Love" and "Poem" toward "a little")

Sometimes my heart goes
all mushy

Remembering good times
we've had

So I thought I would write
you this poem

To say I still love you
like mad

a poem about

Loving

Loving a person is easy
If only you've got the
            right knack
– it's heaping your happiness
All over someone

Who loves heaping
        happiness back

a soppy

Love Poem

Crikey I love you to pieces

My heart wants to jump up
and shout

Let's walk through the
flowers

And huggle for hours

And let all our loveliness
out

big cuddle